POCKET BILLIARDS

POCKET BILLIARDS

Fundamentals of Technique & Play

Bogdan Pejcic & Rolf Meyer

Sterling Publishing Co., Inc.   New York

Translated by Elisabeth E. Reinersmann

Edited by Laurel Ornitz
Editorial Production by Rodman P. Neumann

Library of Congress Cataloging-in-Publication Data
Pejcic, Bogdan.
   [Poolbilliard. English]
   Pocket billiards : fundamentals of technique & play / Bogdan
Pejcic & Rolf Meyer.
     p.   cm.
   Translation of: Poolbilliard.
   Includes index.
   ISBN 0-8069-0458-5
   1. Pool (Game) I. Meyer, Rolf. II. Title.
GV891.P4513   1993
794.7′3—dc20   93-8557
                                           CIP

10 9 8 7

English translation © 1993 by Sterling Publishing Company
387 Park Avenue South, New York, N.Y. 10016
Original edition published under the title
Poolbillard: Grundlagen für Training und Spiel
© 1992 by Falken-Verlag GmbH, 6272 Niedernhausen/Ts.
Distributed in Canada by Sterling Publishing
℅ Canadian Manda Group, P.O. Box 920, Station U
Toronto, Ontario, Canada M8Z 5P9
Distributed in Great Britain and Europe by Cassell PLC
Villiers House, 41/47 Strand, London WC2N 5JE, England
Distributed in Australia by Capricorn Link Ltd.
P.O. Box 704, Windsor, NSW 2756 Australia
Printed in Hong Kong
All rights reserved

Sterling ISBN 0-8069-0458-5

Contents

Contents

Introduction

Pocket billiards requires physical as well as mental stamina. It is a sport that offers fun *and* good fellowship, something not always found in other types of games. It can be played by anybody without a substantial physical limitation. The ever-growing number of billiard halls and clubs has increased the possibilities for people to enjoy this leisure-time activity, regardless of weather conditions.

Pocket billiards has long lost its dubious reputation of simply being a gamblers' game. The German Sports Association elevated pocket billiards to respectability, a status the game has enjoyed in England and America, by holding championship games since the beginning of this century.

The increasing popularity of pocket billiards, or pool, did not start with Paul Newman and Tom Cruise's movie *The Color of Money*. While, over time, membership in the German Pool Billiards Club has grown to 15,000, this rather small number of "officially" recognized players is only a fraction of those people who, in their leisure time, in Germany play pocket billiards day in and day out. The number of people who reach for a cue stick on a regular basis far exceeds two million in the former West German State alone.

The German Pool Billiards Club is involved in the training and licensing of qualified trainers for people seriously interested in the sport.

This book is intended to supplement the club's training program— or any other training program, for that matter—it is not meant to replace a thorough teaching by a trainer or coach. Rather, it is our hope that the book will shed insight on, and broaden your understanding of, the basic elements of pocket billiards. It is also our hope that the book will awaken your curiosity and contribute to your enjoyment.

Characteristics of Billiard Games

Pocket billiards, or pool, refers to any of several games played on a six-pocket table, generally with 15 object balls and a cue ball. Snooker is a pocket-billiards game that is played on a special table with 21 object balls and a cue ball. And carom billiards

Billiard halls are enjoying greater and greater popularity.

applies to any of several games played with three balls on a table without pockets.

The basic skills that are required for pocket billiards are the same as those for Snooker and carom billiards. Among these versions of the sport there are also noticeable similarities in the way players place their hands and feet and the way they hold and use the cue stick.

However, for all these likenesses, the differences that distinguish these games from one another are obvious. For instance, in carom billiards, a player must constantly keep three balls in the game and use different methods of playing them. The idea behind pocket billiards is almost the opposite, because its object is for a player to try as quickly as possible to pocket 15 balls with a cue ball into any one of six pockets positioned around the parameter of the table. In addition, different equipment and differences in concept inevitably lead to differences in the way individual moves are evaluated.

Before You Begin

Tips and Suggestions

Everybody interested in billiards usually has played a game of pool on occasion. Perhaps because a friend invited you to come along, and, after watching the proceedings, you became intrigued, picked up a cue stick, and tried to shoot a ball into a pocket—just as elegantly as you had seen your friend do it. You caught the fever, becoming fascinated by the deliberate way your friend made the balls disappear into the pockets just by hitting the cue ball, often playing off a rail. It is not by accident that pool ranks among the top of all sports in the United States, while the English version of the sport, Snooker, is the undisputed number-one sport on the charts on the British Isles—way ahead of soccer! In fact, pocket billiards has advanced to one of the most favored leisure-time activities and competitive sports all over the world—and it is easy to understand why: the game's accessibility and quick, easily observable results, as well as its competitive character, not only against an opponent but also against oneself.

Pocket billiards has long since shed its reputation of being a somewhat shady, back-room game of luck. Professional players in the United States, but also in England, Japan, Indonesia, and the Philippines, are earning healthy sums of money at this "sport at the green table." In addition, millions of amateurs in these countries of all ages and both genders have been attracted to this sport. And, in German-speaking countries, pocket billiards has developed into a leisure-time activity that is enjoyed by the whole family.

No matter how fascinated and inspired you become during your first attempt at this game, it probably didn't take you long to realize that the balls usually didn't go where you intended them to. They most likely seemed to lose their good position on the table, a position from which you thought it would be a cinch to shoot them into a pocket. The cue ball, more often than not, either moved too far, or not far enough; or it hit a colored ball at the wrong spot, or, even worse, the cue ball itself disappeared in a pocket. "Too bad," you might have muttered, "bad luck." However, these are typical beginner's mistakes, but it would be a good idea not to let these mistakes become bad habits.

9

Don't pull your hair out when a shot does not bring your anticipated result. Mistakes are a normal part of the learning process. But mistakes are only beneficial when you try to learn from them.

Prerequisites

Generally speaking, pocket billiards is a sport that everybody can learn. If you practise consistently, you will soon discover that, in addition to a certain amount of physical stamina, what is required for playing this game is a measure of aptitude, maximum concentration, and a certain amount of intuition. Sooner or later, you will want to have a strategy for maximizing the effectiveness of your shots, pocketing as many balls as possible. This book will help you understand the "physics" involved in moving balls around and making you a better player—because nothing in billiards is a matter of chance.

You will learn the basic elements of the game, how to hold and use the cue stick, and how this affects your shots; what's more, you will find suggestions on how to practise and how to improve your game.

Take note of these suggestions, and practise the recommended exercises as often as possible. You will notice that, over time, your "feel" for the game will get better and better.

Approach your practice sessions on two fronts: Play as many practice games as time permits (in the beginning, it is best to play straight pool), but make sure that you focus sufficiently on specifics, like your stroke, banking, and solving particular situations.

Here is another important tip we would like to pass on to you right from the beginning: If at all possible, try to find an experienced player as a partner. Only an experienced player can make you aware of your mistakes—for instance, of the way you may be holding and using the cue stick to your disadvantage—correct them, and give you useful tips. If you should find an experienced coach, do not hesitate to train with him or her. But, in the absence of such an opportunity, a professional billiards player or a more advanced player at a billiards club would probably be more than willing to answer your questions or give you advice.

Learning the Basics

Equipment

We know of very few other games in which success depends so much on not only the skill of the player but also on the quality of the equipment that is used. A billiard table that is not level, which has rails that are too soft or too hard; poorly balanced balls; and crooked cue sticks, will always affect your game. But, even if everything is as it should be, it is important for players to have solid knowledge about the equipment they are using. This applies not only to the cue stick, but also to the balls they are moving around as well as to the table on which they are playing.

The Table

Simply stated, the billiard table consists of a frame, the tabletop, and cushioned edges, or the rails. In the past, the tops of billiard tables were made from solid, very expensive marble. With the increase in the game's popularity, the marble was replaced by slate. Today, three slate plates of equal thickness are joined to produce the tabletop. The leather-covered boards that were mounted around the table in order to contain the balls have been replaced by rails made of hard rubber that should be of equal elasticity all around. Depending on their manufacturer, the rails will differ in their degree of softness or hardness.

The softer the rail, the greater the difference between the angle of approach and the angle of completion of the ball. A player should take this into consideration when playing on a "foreign" table. The direction and speed of a ball played off the rail might be different from that on a familiar table.

Both the rails and the surface of the table are covered with a tightly woven wool cloth. You should not be able to move the cloth when you place your hand flat on the table and try to move across the surface. It goes without saying that the cover should be flawless, as any wrinkles or dents would interfere with the movement of the balls. High-quality cloth also allows a player the most minute ball movements. Therefore, make sure that the cover of the table is smooth.

A ball will move faster on a smooth surface because there is less resistance. The same amount of force will make a ball roll faster and far-

A billiard table in impeccable condition is a basic requirement for precision play.

ther when the surface is smooth than when it is rough or felt-like. In Europe, billiard tables are usually covered with smooth cloth, while, in the United States, where pocket billiards originated, the felt-like cloth is used. The color of the cloth is also important. Sometimes the color of the covers is turquoise or blue. This might look rather attractive on first sight; however, over the long haul, these colors will strain your eyes. Green, however, is a soothing color.

Table Size

The proportional size of the playing surface of a billiard table is standard, with a ratio of 2 to 1.

The basic sizes are 4 feet by 8 feet and 4½ feet by 9 feet; the height in both cases is from 31 to 32 inches.

Markings

Two markings—one each in the upper and lower thirds of the table— identify the head and the foot of the table, respectively, and are called the foot marker and the head marker. The vertical line—parallel to the long side rails and through the foot marker—serve as a guide for replacing wrongly pocketed balls back on the table. The first ball is put on the foot marker, subsequent misplayed balls are put on the foot line towards the foot rail, and frozen balls are put behind the line. The horizontal line through the head marker—parallel to the head rail—is called the head line and identifies the head field.

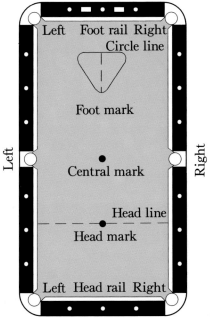

The markings on a pocket billiard table.

At the start of every game, balls are placed on the table by means of a wooden or plastic rack generally in the shape of a triangle, with the ball in the tip of the triangle pointing towards the head of the table positioned on the foot marker. The exception are balls for a Nine Ball game, which are arranged in a rhombus shape. Breaking is done from the head of the table.

The rails on most tables are marked with diamond-shaped inlays, which serve as orientation markers for cross-rail shots.

Good billiard lounges and clubs will provide sufficient space around each table to prevent players from interfering with players on neighboring tables.

Billiard Balls

In the past, billiard balls were made from the finest and most expensive material. While the marble tabletop alone could represent an enormous investment, purchasing balls would burden one's budget even more. "Real" billiard balls were once made from pure ivory. Balls made from wood and metal were always available, but using them to make a successful shot was more a matter of luck than the skill of the player. Until the invention of high-quality plastic, used to make most billiard balls to-

*Solid-colored balls, numbers one through seven,
and the black ball, number eight.*

day, ivory was the only guarantee that a ball would be perfectly round and the center of gravity would be at the geometrical center. Both of these criteria are crucial for a successful billiards game. If the point of gravity is off-center and you have a "crooked" ball, the greatest technical skills become useless, turning a game into a chance of luck. The change in the material used to make billiard balls was not so much due to a desire to protect the elephant as to the development of modern and affordable manufacturing methods and materials, such as phenolic resin.

Pocket-billiard balls are 2.25 inches in diameter and weigh 5.5 ounces. The white ball is called the cue ball or simply the "white" ball. This is the only ball used to make a shot. The rest of the 15 balls, the so-called "colored" balls, are divided into two groups: solid-color balls, numbered from one to seven, and striped balls, numbered from nine to fifteen. In addition, there is a black ball with the number eight on it, a ball that has special significance for the Eight Ball game.

Striped balls, numbers nine through fifteen.

The Cue Stick

In billiards, in most instances, the table and the balls are a given — players must be content with what is in front of them. But this is not so when it comes to the cue stick. In this case, players can make choices and use what suits them best.

Various types of cue sticks are available: one-piece cue sticks, which are usually found at bars, pool halls, and billiard clubs, and jointed cue sticks, which are, in general, the personal property of a player. The latter have a distinct advantage because they can be easily transported. Some cue sticks at certain bars and clubs have very little in common with a normal cue stick other than the name. A quick glance usually is all that is needed to detect poor workmanship. Reputable pool halls and clubs, on the other hand, have, in addition to several tables (with different cloth covers), a fairly impressive array of cues. At such establishments, every player can choose "his"

or "her" cue, and a beginner can inexpensively experiment with several different sticks. Sooner or later, you might want to own your own cue. But before running out to the nearest store, it is best to first experiment with several different cue sticks, which you can do at these places.

Length and weight are the determining factors for the "right" cue, and different players have different needs. While the length averages around 55 inches, weight is another matter. On an average, the weight of a cue stick ranges from 17 to 22 ounces. For the beginner, we recommend a weight of about 19 ounces. A cue that is too heavy often results in a hit that is much stronger than the player had intended it to be; if too light, on the other hand, guiding it with a straight, steady stroke becomes difficult, often causing the tip of the cue to slip off the cue ball.

Many cue sticks have a removable rubber cap into which different weights can be inserted. This makes it easy to individually adjust the

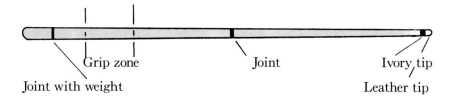

Diagram of a cue stick used to play pocket billiards.

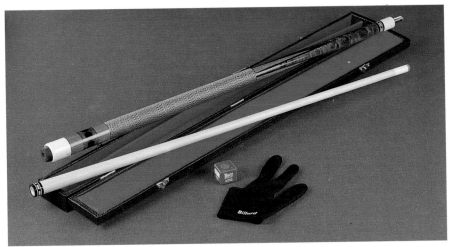

Basic equipment: jointed cue stick, with case, chalk, and gloves.

weight of the stick, since requirements will change as a player gains more experience.

Most cues today are made from wood from Canadian maple, with varying degrees of elasticity. Cues from softer wood are a better choice for making more complicated shots and shooting spin balls. The latest trend on the market is wooden cues with a fibreglass covering. This new development has a great advantage in that it is easier to keep the tip clean, since even the most carefully handled cue stick becomes soiled over time, making cleaning the tip a necessity. To clean wooden tips, you need to sand them with sandpaper. However, sanding will eventually wear them down and thus interfere with your ability to shoot straight. Sooner or later, the tip on the cue stick has to be replaced. However, this problem has been eliminated with the new fibreglass covering.

Those who have tried their hand at Three-Cushion Billiards no doubt have noticed that the cue sticks used for pool are lighter and shorter than those used for playing carom-billiard games. The latter are evenly tapered from the tip on down to the end, whereas, with pocket-billiard cues, only the first 12 inches or so are tapered.

This is necessary because, in pocket billiards, the distance between the left hand (the bridge hand) and the cue ball must be greater. The player has more room for his or her stroke and can more easily adjust the amount of force he or she wants to apply to the cue ball.

Just as the length and weight of the cue stick can vary, so can the diameter of the tip. The average diameter is between ⅜ and ½ inch. Which is better—a narrow or wider tip? Both have their advantages. Aiming is easier with a tip that is narrower; a wider tip, on the other hand, increases the point of contact and thereby improves the transfer of power. Test which one serves your particular play best.

The end of the tip is covered with a fairly soft patch of leather. The connection between the tip and the shaft is called the ferrule. As with billiard balls in the past, the ferrule was made of ivory. Although you still can see ivory on very expensive cues today, now most ferrules are made from plastic. How hard or soft the leather covering is on the tip is a matter of personal preference. However, leather tips that are glued on are better than those that are screwed on (piloted joints), if, for no other reason, than expense. In addition, a cue stick with a piloted joint has metal parts that pose a danger of damaging the table cover when the tip wears down.

Chalk is applied to the tip frequently during the course of a game, particularly when making off-center shots. Chalk helps prevent the tip from slipping off the ball.

At the end of the cue is the grip, which could either be lacquered or covered with cloth. In the final analysis, this portion determines the price of the cue. Manufacturers like to give luxurious touches to the grip of the cue stick by adding either amber, gold, or ivory inlays to the wood or by applying expensive lacquer by means of complicated procedures. However, such additions will quickly raise the price of a cue into four- or five-figure numbers. Pocket billiards, however,

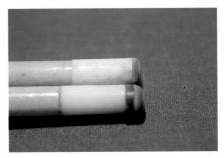

Here are two examples of what a bad tip looks like.

Here is a well-cared-for tip.

When your arm is too short, reach for a mechanical bridge.

is for many not just a leisure-time activity but rather a passion and a profession; for those among us who belong to this group, having the "best" equipment becomes a matter of course.

The Mechanical Bridge

When none of the hand bridges will allow you to reach the cue ball, a mechanical bridge can be useful. Mechanical bridges generally have several ridges of different heights; choose the ridge that provides the best support. However, a mechanical bridge should only be used in rare situations, because using it properly depends on a high level of experience. Always check carefully whether a ball cannot be played just as well by using the hand bridge—maybe off the rail.

Stance

Proper stance is one of the most important factors in the game of billiards. Not until you have learned proper body posture, combined with a confident stroke and accurate aim, can you hope to shoot effectively. Although we do not have an exact formula, it would be to the advantage of beginners to familiarize themselves with a few basic rules and avoid getting into bad habits. The following guidelines are meant for right-handed players; nevertheless, they can be followed in reverse by left-handed players—and every player should practise from both sides, the left and the right hand, from the very beginning.

Keeping your eye on the ball is the best position from which to aim accurately.

Body Posture and Aim

Your stance should be relaxed, with both feet planted solidly on the ground. Feet are about a shoulder-width apart, with the left foot slightly in front of the right foot and the body at an angle of about 45 degrees to the vertical axis of the cue. The upper body should lean over, bending at the hips; the chin and eyes should be over the cue stick. This is the best position for successfully aiming the ball.

Holding the Cue Stick and Aiming

The success of a shot depends on the quality of your aim and your stroke. The right hand holds and guides the cue stick. Hold, or rather cradle, the cue stick in your right hand at the grip at a point approximately halfway between the end of the cue and its center of gravity. Don't let your thumb rest on top of the cue stick; it will needlessly cause your wrist to tense up, which in turn will interfere with a relaxed, easy stroke. Of course, the position of the cue hand will depend also on the position of the cue ball. The farther the ball is away from the rail, the farther you must stretch in order to reach it. When the ball is far away, your right hand will grip the cue stick more towards the end of the cue than would be the case

19

The starting position should be the following: upper and lower right arm relaxed, forming a 90-degree angle, with the cue stick cradled in the hand.

if the cue ball is closer to the rail, where the cue ball can only be hit when you raise the end of the cue stick. While striking the cue ball, your eyes should concentrate on the point where you intend to make contact with the object ball.

Basically, the right arm should bend at the elbow at a 90-degree an-

gle. The stroke originates from the elbow joint.

The wrist and underside of the arm, for the left hand, form a straight line. If the wrist is bent either to the left or right, the contact point between the tip of the cue stick and the cue ball will shift one way or the other. The entire cue stick, from the

20

When a shot is correctly executed, the wrist and underside of the arm form a straight line.

This is the wrong way of holding the cue.

butt to the tip, must be viewed as an extension of the direction of the intended stroke, or it must form a parallel line to it.

If the cue stick is held incorrectly from the outset, the ball will move in the wrong direction. One of the most frequent mistakes beginners make, without even being aware of it, is

making stirring motions with the cue stick, which causes side moves.

Any arm movement should always be preceded by quiet contemplation. Any hectic back-and-forth movements will only be transferred to the actual stroke and, in most cases, guarantee a missed or wrong shot.

The cue is an extension of the direction of the stroke; here, before (left) and after (right) the shot.

Bridges

The left hand is used as support for the cue, forming what is called the bridge. It is intended to stabilize the cue stick, preventing it from slipping and causing an inaccurate shot. Depending on the situation of the game, several different bridges of varying height can be used. The height is determined by the way you position your fingers and the ball of your hand on the surface of the table. Which position to use depends on the position of the cue ball. For instance, is the ball close to the rail or more towards the middle of the table, or is the ball easy to reach or crowded by other balls? The ideal distance between the bridge hand and the cue ball is about 5 to 7 inches.

It is important to make sure that this distance is neither too great nor too small, even when the position of the object ball to be pocketed and the necessary stroke seem to suggest otherwise. Always try to guide the cue as low and parallel to the table surface as possible. It guarantees accurate aim and lets you choose the best point of impact on the object ball. A cue held too high, with the exception of special shots, like the jump shot, increases the chances of a miscue.

One rule applies to every type of bridge: The more stable the left hand is on the surface of the table, the more accurate your stroke will be.

Closed Bridge

The closed bridge could be called the "standard bridge." The middle, ring, and small fingers, as well as the ball of the hand, are securely placed on the surface of the table. The fingers are spread apart for stability. The index finger, forming a ring, touches the thumb. The "ring" serves as the guide for the cue, which is resting on the middle finger. This is the most secure way of guiding the cue because it is practically impossible for it to slide off.

The closed bridge.

The open bridge above the ball.

Open Bridge

You will not always be able to make use of the closed, or standard, bridge. Often the cue ball is too close either to the object ball or the rail. In such situations, it is best to use the open bridge. The tips of the four fingers form the support for the hand. The thumb is spread upwards, and the cue rests between the thumb and index finger. It goes without saying that this method requires the player to be in command of guiding the cue stick with a steady stroke.

Another variation of the open bridge is the low, flat bridge, in which all four fingers (including the ball of the small finger) provide the anchor. This bridge is often used for back spins.

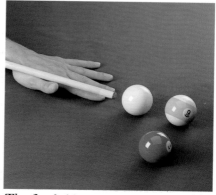

The flat bridge.

Rail Bridges

A rail bridge is used when the cue ball is relatively close to the rail. The rail serves as the support, and the cue is guided between the index and middle fingers (see left photo, below). Some players use a closed fist when the cue stick must be held at a steep angle. The tip of the cue rests in the indentation between the knuckles (see photo on the right, top).

Another possibility for hitting rail shots or shots that require height is the following bridge: Rest your hand flat on the table surface with fingers closed. The index finger is slightly raised, but its tip remains on the surface of the table. Angle the thumb towards the palm of your hand, moving it away from the index finger. This will create a "resting" place that is used as a guide for the cue, which is in an almost parallel position to the table. This bridge allows you to execute your shot without any problems (see photo lower right).

Here is another important tip: From the very beginning, you can never be too vigilant in trying to ac-

The closed fist for shots that require height.

The rail bridge.

The bridge for low, flat shots.

The proper stance and a secure guide for the cue stick are the basics for a successful game.

quire the correct position for your cue stick and a steady stroke. Constantly having to check and correct these things might be tiresome and a bother, but it will be to your advantage in the long run. During the course of a game, it is imperative to observe and calculate as many techniques and tactics as possible. Your concentration should be focused on the situation on the table, and you should always think ahead, contemplating the strategy for your next shot. It is here where having practised the correct stance and a steady, secure stroke starts to pay off. Right from the start, double-check stance and hand position prior to executing a shot. When aiming, look beyond the tip of the cue. Make several warm-up strokes, at a speed you actually intend to use. This will give you a good sense of the intensity of your stroke before actually hitting the cue ball. The very last warm-up move should stop just short of the cue ball; this lets you check your stroke and "see" the point of impact on the cue ball.

Shooting

Probably you have already had some experience playing pocket billiards. Most likely, when making your first attempts at hitting the balls, you watched them travel an entirely different path than you had anticipated.

25

Undoubtedly, this had very little to do with an accident or bad luck, as you might have tried to tell yourself.

Each shot in a game is the result of a chain of events that, at least in theory, can be calculated rather precisely beforehand. One of the links in this chain of events is the stroke that determines not only the direction of a ball's movement but also the way in which it moves. The way a ball moves after impact and the way it behaves after it has struck a rail are important subjects in this chapter. Some of you might argue that such theoretical discussions are useless. However, if you understand the underlying principles at work and know them well, they will be available to you at all times. If you lack the knowledge of the different shooting methods, the effect they have on the behavior of the ball, and how a ball reacts when played off a rail, pocket billiards will forever remain a game of "chance" or "luck."

Point of Impact, Point of Contact, Direction of Stroke

The point where the tip of the cue stick hits the cue ball is called the "point of impact"; it is here where the transfer of force or energy from the stroke to the cue ball takes place. The point where two balls meet is called the "point of contact." "Direction of stroke" is the extension of the horizontal axis of the cue stick at the moment when the ball was hit, either dead center (straight-on) or off to the side.

It is easy to practise straight shots; here, one is shown with the aid of an empty bottle.

Types of Strokes

A line drawn from the upper to the lower poles and from the left to the right sides of a ball will mark the middle and give you vertical and horizontal coordinates.

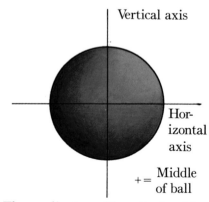

The coordinates, with vertical and horizontal axes and central point.

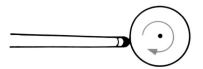

A ball turning around its horizontal axis.

The middle of the ball is the point at which the two coordinates meet and also its center of gravity. A straight-on shot will result in the ball turning around its horizontal axis. Striking off to the side will turn the ball around its vertical axis, and, thus, the ball will remain where it is.

The horizontal and vertical midlines create the "cross hair." Use this cross hair to calculate your shots.

Shots that are aimed above or below the horizontal line are called high and low shots, respectively. Likewise, shots aimed at the left or right of the vertical line are called right and left shots, respectively.

Straight-On Shot

This is considered the basic shot, and its mastery is the basis for all other variations. (This shot is also called the frontal or center shot.)

The point of contact is aimed exactly at the middle of the cross hair, where the direction of the stroke travels horizontally through the central point of the ball. This shot will result in a simple rotation of the ball around its horizontal axis.

The straight-on shot.

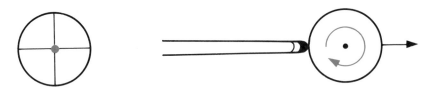

When the point of contact is the middle of the ball, the ball simply turns around its horizontal axis.

Immediately following the impact, the ball will first slide a little before it starts to roll, which is due to the resistance created by the friction between the cloth cover and the movement of the ball. The distance the ball will travel depends on the force of the stroke. This might be a good time to point out that the force of the stroke is not only influenced by the length of the distance travelled by the cue stick but also by the amount of time the cue ball and object ball are in contact. Strike the cue ball as if you wanted to penetrate the cue stick through the middle of the ball.

When the cue ball hits the object ball straight-on, the cue ball will continue to follow the movement of the object ball for a distance; how far will depend on the force of the shot. Moving the point of impact above or below the middle point results in two variations of the straight-on shot: the forward spin and the back spin.

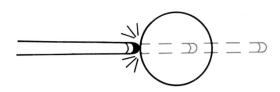

With a straight-on shot, the cue is literally aimed to shoot straight through the cue ball.

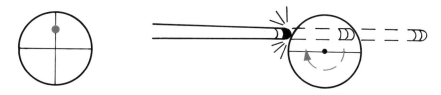

When the point of contact is above the middle of the ball, a forward spin is created.

Forward Spin

The force created when ball A strikes ball B carries A forward; then A will follow in the path of B. This is possible because of the forward spin put on ball A, since the cue stick struck the ball above the middle. Due to the forward spin, after ball A has struck ball B, ball A has enough force left so that the momentum continues to carry it forward, following the path of ball B. The higher on the vertical line the cue makes contact, the stronger the spin will be, but less momentum will carry the ball forward.

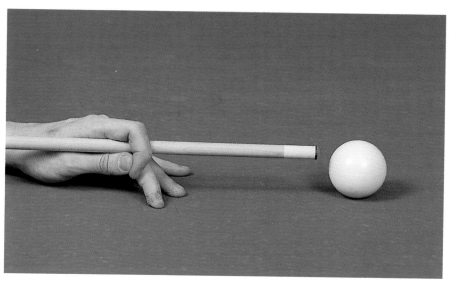

Forward spin.

Back spin.

Back Spin

The behavior of a ball with a back spin is the exact opposite from that of a ball with a forward spin. The cue ball is hit below the middle, which also drives it forward while putting a backward spin on it. The sliding path is longer for a back-spin shot than for a forward-spin or straight-on shot. The back spin does not begin until contact with the object ball has been made, which interrupts the forward movement.

This shot is used when the player wants to return the cue ball in the direction of its original position. It is not an easy shot, and two factors must be taken into consideration: the back spin and the path the ball is to take during its forward movement. If the distance of the forward movement is too long and the shot is too weak, the ball might lose its spin. The friction created by the ball moving across the cloth might create enough resistance to slow down the movement.

Beginners should first try to use the back spin only across short distances and with straight-on shots. Only after these are mastered should they attempt to play balls that are in different and more difficult positions.

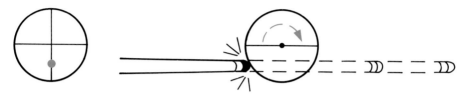

When the point of impact is below the middle of the ball, a back spin is created.

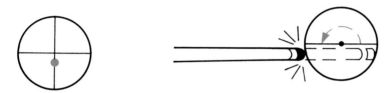

When the point of impact is below the middle of the ball, as for the back spin, but the ball is hit with a quick, hard stroke, a stop ball is created.

Stop Ball

If the cue ball is to remain on the spot where it struck the intended object ball, the "stop ball," a variation of the back spin, is used. The point of impact is below the middle of the ball, and the cue hits the ball with a quick and hard stroke. As with the back spin, in the beginning this shot should only be attempted over short distances. Only after the technique has been mastered can the shot be used over longer distances.

Stop ball.

31

English

All shots discussed so far were hit on the "vertical line," which resulted in a spinning impulse around the horizontal axis. In the case of "English," however, the ball is struck either left or right of its central point. This results in the ball spinning around the vertical axis.

If the point of impact is on the right side of the ball, the spin will be counterclockwise. This English shot is also simply called right spin. In reverse, if the ball is struck left of its central point, a clockwise spin is initiated, called a left spin. The farther away from the middle the point of impact, the stronger the spin, but, at the same time, the slower the forward movement.

The rule for forward and back spins as well as for English shots— the left and right spins—is that the farther away from the middle point a ball is hit, the stronger is its spin, the weaker is the impact, and, consequently, the slower the forward movement of the ball. An optimum spinning speed is achieved by staying within the radius of the ball.

It is also important to note that balls that are struck for English will move slightly to the side in which the ball is spinning. A left-spin ball,

therefore, will move slightly more to the right; a right-spin ball will move slightly more to the left. This has to be taken into consideration when aiming and must be compensated for.

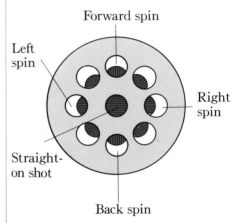

The "ball clock" shows the point at which the ball has to be struck in order to create the different spins.

12 o'clock = for a forward-spin shot
3 o'clock = for a right-spin shot
6 o'clock = for a back-spin shot
9 o'clock = for a left-spin shot

Circles that are not identified in the "ball clock" represent combination shots. The circles within the clock show the precise points at which a player must aim, with the red portion indicating the area of contact between the tip of the cue stick and the surface of the ball.

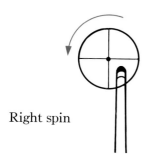
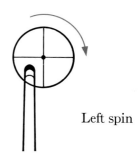

Right spin

Left spin

Direction of spin, and point where the ball has to be struck for right- and left-spin shots, respectively.

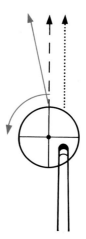

Direction of movement of a ball with spin
Direction of movement of straight-on shot
Direction of movement of cue

Change in direction of movement of ball with spin versus direction of aim.

Banking and Caroms

In the previous sections, we discussed the different methods of striking a ball and the effects they have on its rotation. Now we want to look at the different ways a ball moves—particularly after it has struck a rail or another ball. It is here where we will learn about the real impact of the different shots we use.

Ball Movement after Hitting a Rail

The angle at which a ball moves towards the rail is called the "angle of approach"; the angle at which the ball leaves the rail is called the "angle of completion." Everything is viewed from the player's perspective or the tip of the cue stick.

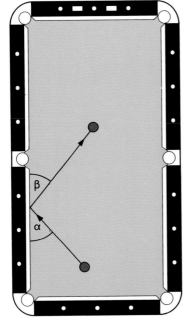

Behavior of a ball after it has hit a rail.

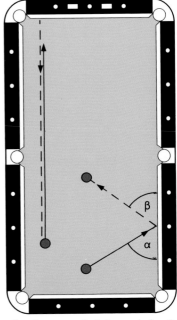

Angle of approach (α) = angle of completion (β), with a straight-on shot.

Banking with Straight-On Shots

A straight-on shot hitting the rail vertically will return on the same path. The only change that has taken place is the reversal of the direction of the spin of the ball around its horizontal axis. This reversal happens after the ball hits the rail. The angle of approach and the angle of completion are identical: 90 degrees. This holds true even if the ball is played at an angle, provided a straight-on shot is

used! The ball leaves the rail at the same angle at which it approached it (angle of approach equals angle of completion).

However, there can be no rules without exceptions. Since today's rails are made almost entirely of materials that are very elastic, a rail transfers the energy of the impact with which the ball is hitting it back to the ball. With a straight-on shot, this transfer of energy is essentially total. However, when the ball is shot to the rail at an angle, the energy created through the impact is not uniform. Consequently, the rail does not reflect the energy completely, as would be the case with the straight-on shot. Depending on the speed, the angle of completion may differ slightly. A forceful shot will result in a wider angle; a lighter, softer shot will decrease the angle. The deviation, however, while important to consider, is minimal and should not be compared to the effect a ball with English has when it hits the rail.

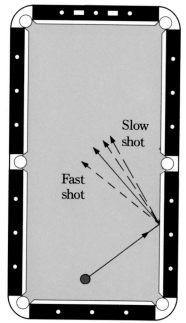

Transfer of energy.

Banking and Balls with English

Only banking and, to a lesser extent, caroms bring out the full effect of English. A right-spin ball played vertically against a rail will not assume a straight path after the impact but will move to the right, in contrast to a straight-on shot. The same, in reverse, holds true for a left-spin ball. How much a ball will move to the right—or left—will depend on the run as well as the speed of rotation, or the strength of its spin. The greater the rotation, the smaller the angle of completion, and vice versa.

When a ball is not played straight-on, the difference in the angle of completion will depend on which side the cue ball has been struck and where it has hit the rail. For instance, if a left-spin ball is played against the right rail, the angle of completion will be less than the angle of approach. At the same time, the speed of a ball is increased through the contact it makes with the rail. In such cases, we are talking about a "co-effect." This

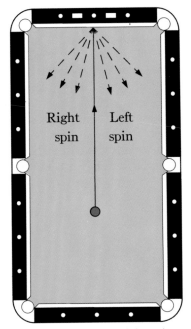

Banking with left and right spins.

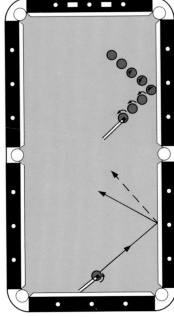

Co-effect.

co-effect can be explained as follows: The ball at the moment of impact, because of its spin, will run in the direction of the rail. "Counter-effect" is the opposite: The angle of completion is greater than the angle of approach when a right-spin ball is played off the right rail. In this case, the spin of the ball is running against the rail, the rail is breaking the speed of the ball, and the ball leaves the rail at a steeper angle. Just as with the straight-on shot, the more power, the greater the spin and the larger the

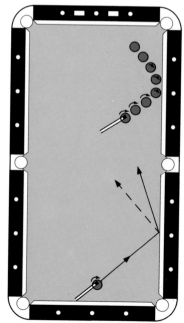

Counter-effect.

deviation. When playing off several rails, the spin remains unaltered; still, the distance the ball will travel and the impact on the rail are reduced.

Ball Behavior in Caroms after Rail Impact

We have already discussed the different methods of hitting a ball and the two ways a ball behaves after it has been hit in the case of the forward spin and the back spin. But what are the other ways that a carom affects billiard balls after impact? The result of contact between a moving (cue) ball and static (object) balls depends on what type of hit has set the ball in motion, the path the ball travels, and the force of the hit. An object ball may be hit straight-on or on either side of the midline. Such a ball will travel in a straight line—a line that is the extension of the line from the point of contact through its central point. The angle created by the two different paths—the one the cue ball travels and the different path the object ball will travel—is called the "angle of approach," which is 0 degrees in the case of a straight-on shot and 30 degrees in the case of a half-straight-on shot. At the same time, the path that the cue ball travels will also change depending on where the ball was hit and if it had English. The angle between the new path (of the object ball) and the old path (of

37

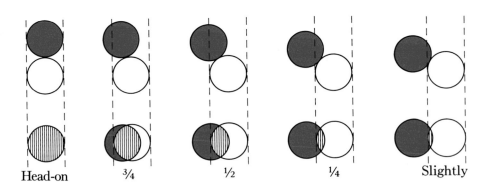

| Head-on | ¾ | ½ | ¼ | Slightly |

Point of contact between cue ball (white) and object ball (red).

the cue ball) is called the "angle of continuation." Both the angle of approach and angle of continuation will always be 90 degrees when using a straight-on shot. This means that the more head-on the object ball has been hit, the smaller the angle of approach will be and the larger the angle of continuation. In other words, the more directly a ball is hit, the less its path will diverge from that of the cue ball and the wider the angle of approach of the cue ball will be. Likewise, the wider the angle of approach, the less likely it is for the cue ball to lose speed after impact.

The angle of continuation for English is different from that for a straight-on shot. If the hit is on the side of the angle of approach—in other words, on the same side to which the object ball will move—this angle will be smaller than it would be with a straight-on shot. If the cue ball is hit on the outside, the angle of continuation will be wider.

At the same time, the English of the cue ball will be transferred to the object ball in the opposite direction. Very little friction is created when contact is made between the balls since their surfaces are smooth. The spin that is transferred to the object ball (forward spin and back spin) is therefore less than that of the cue ball.

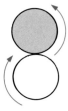

Transfer of spin.

38

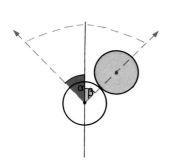 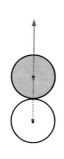 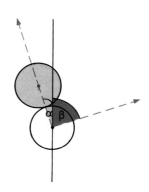

$\alpha + \beta = 90$ degrees   Straight-on shot   Half-shot

$\alpha = 0$ degrees, $\beta = 0$ degrees $\alpha + \beta = 90$ degrees

Reaction of ball after impact (straight-on shot);
$\alpha = $ *angle of approach and* $\beta = $ *angle of continuation.*

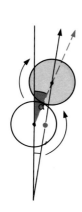 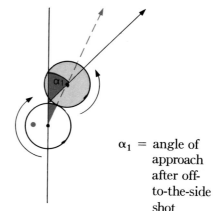

$\alpha_1 = $ angle of approach after off-to-the-side shot

Reaction of ball after off-to-the-side shot.

- - - → = straight-on shot
——→ = direction of new path

Practising Straight-On Shots

Practising Techniques

After having discussed the different shots—straight-on, forward spin, back spin, stop ball, and English—and the way the balls move, especially after contact, it is time to venture into the wide-open field of actual practice. What we try to do here is give you an overview of the many different possibilities and variations that can be found in real game situations. What follows are presentations of a variety of standard situations, which, we hope, will help you in thinking up all kinds of other game situations for yourself.

At first, some of the exercises may seem very simple, but you will soon discover that they are more difficult than you thought. In the beginning, try to use the straight-on shot for all exercises. For exercises 1 through 11, place the cue ball anywhere you want.

Many beginners make the error of hitting the cue ball too hard. They are under the mistaken notion that hitting the cue ball hard will make

pocketing an object ball easier. What they fail to realize is that, in the very process of hitting hard, their cue stick moves farther, which in itself is the source of many mistakes. You also need to pay attention to stance and cue position, and to making sure that you cradle the stick gently in your hand; do not hold on to the cue stick too tightly.

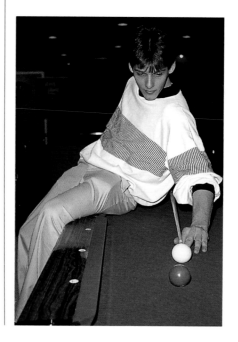

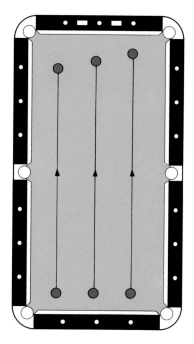

Exercise 1.

Practising Straight-On Shots and Force of Stroke

Exercise 1
Practise hitting the ball gently and softly. Play the cue ball from the foot rail to the head rail, trying to make the ball come to rest as close to the head rail as possible.

Exercise 2
Position the cue ball so that you will be able to hit the opposite rail as comfortably as possible. Now, using the

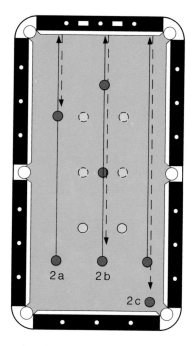

Exercises 2 and 3.

straight-on shot (middle of the ball), shoot the ball vertically towards the opposite rail so that the ball will travel back the identical path (2a).

A more difficult variation is what is called the "alley run." Here, the ball is supposed to move through one or more pairs of balls and then move back the same way (2b). Now you will discover that when a ball is hit more gently and is moving at a slower speed, you will see much better results than when the ball is hit hard.

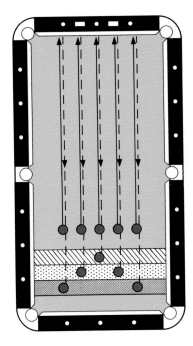

Exercise 4.

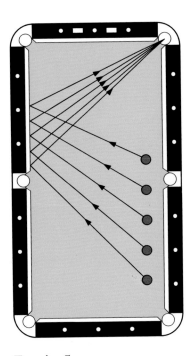

Exercise 5.

Exercise 3

Here, again, use the straight-on shot. This time the stroke should be strong enough so that the momentum carries the ball back to the foot rail as close as possible (2c). This is an important exercise since it involves practising skills that you will need for successful breaking at the beginning of the game.

Exercise 4

Divide the table surface into different zones (either with chalk or, if you prefer, strips of paper). Again, using straight-on shots, now try to place the ball in any one of the zones, playing off one or more rails. What follow are two variations of this exercise.

Place several balls in a row. Now try to place each ball into a different zone. The pattern should be determined beforehand.

This is a more difficult version: Instead of chalk lines or strips of paper, use little game pieces, like those used in Chinese checkers. Try to play the cue ball so that it comes to rest immediately in front of the game pieces—without knocking them

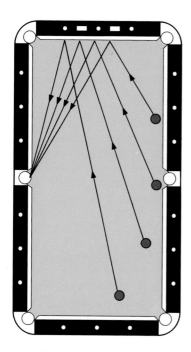

Exercise 5 (continued).

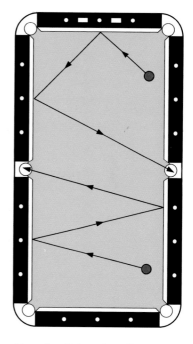

Exercise 5 (continued).

over. If you practise this with a part-ner, it can become a competitive game: Who can bring the cue ball to rest closest to the game piece?

Exercise 5

We will stay with the straight-on shot. Up until now, we have played the rail with vertical shots. Now we want to try to play the rails on an angle. When playing French billiards (carom billiards), angle shots are a must; whereas, in pocket billiards, they are always full of risks and should only be used when there are no other options.

Using the straight-on shot, try to pocket your ball by playing off the rail. Use the diamonds—markers in the rail—if your table has them, as points of orientation. Test your shots, using different bridges, aiming to-wards different pockets, and hitting across several rails.

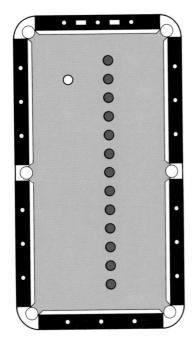

Exercise 6.

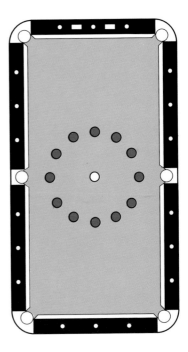

Exercise 7.

Practising with a Second Ball

The following exercises are an introduction to caroms.

Exercise 6
Pocket every red ball on the table; however, the cue ball is not to touch any of the other red balls. If you make a mistake, start all over again.

Exercise 7
Here, too, the object is to pocket every ball. But the cue ball may not leave the circle. The circle stays intact by putting each ball back in its original place after every successful shot.

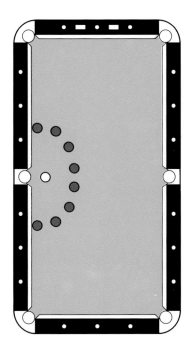

Exercise 8.

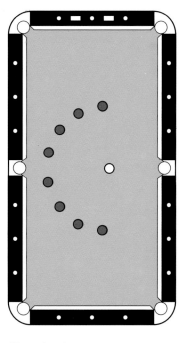

Exercise 9.

Exercise 8
Pocket every red ball without the cue ball leaving the half-circle or touching any of the other red balls. The sequence in which the balls are played is left up to you.

Exercise 9
Pocket every red ball into the side pocket. Here, too, the rules are that you can play in any sequence you like and the cue ball cannot touch any other ball but the object ball.

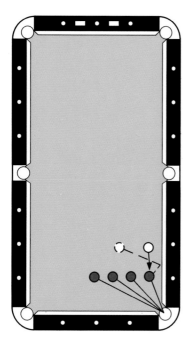

Exercise 10.

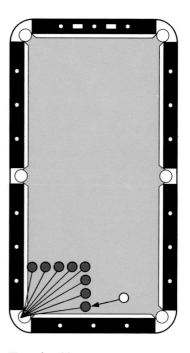

Exercise 11.

Exercise 10

All four red balls are to be pocketed —
playing from above. To increase the
degree of difficulty, try bringing the
cue ball — after it has hit the rail and
pocketed a ball — into a position from
which to play the next ball (see bro-
ken line on drawing).

Exercise 11

Hit every red ball into the corner
pocket, in any sequence you choose.

Practice Banking

Up until now, you have practised pocketing every ball directly into a pocket. This is the basic technique that should be used whenever possible. Playing off of a rail with English might look intriguing, but it also carries many more risks. A straight-on shot, played directly, may look somewhat boring, but, in most cases, it will be much more successful than the exotic shot off of a rail or with English.

However, time and again you will be presented with situations in which you must play with English or off a rail. It could be that an opponent's ball is blocking you or that there is a good chance of pocketing the cue ball with a colored ball.

In order to be prepared for such situations, the play off the rail should be practised just as much as straight-on shots. This goes for pre-contact, in which the cue ball hits the rail once or even several times before it makes contact with the object ball(s), as well as after-impact. As you go through the following exercises, practise using accurate aim and the proper amount of force.

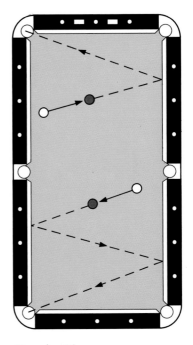

Exercise 12.

Exercise 12

Try, from different positions on the table, to pocket the red ball, using straight-on shots, playing the red ball across the rails.

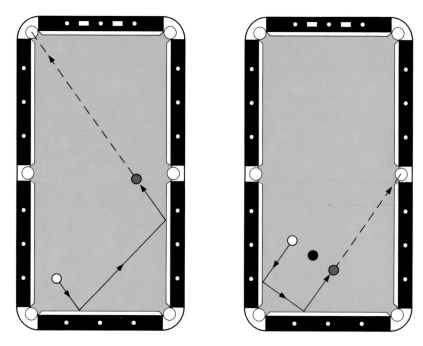

Exercise 12 (continued).

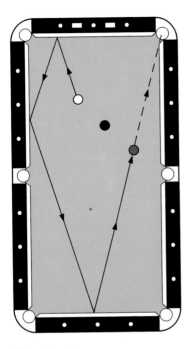

Exercise 13.

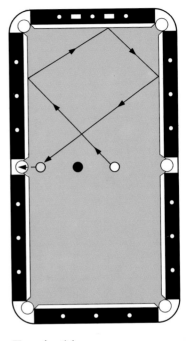

Exercise 14.

Exercise 13

Indirect pocketing: Position your "opponent's" ball in such a way that it blocks direct access to your object ball and thereby forces you to play off several rails.

Exercise 14

This is a different approach for indirect pocketing, with a similar setup using double-banking.

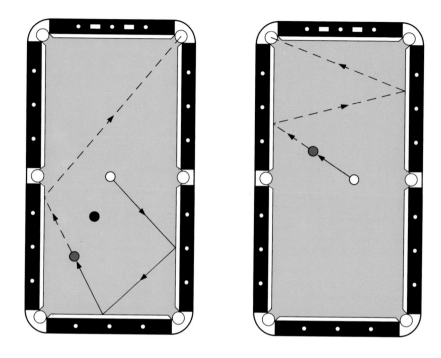

Exercises 13 and 14 (continued).

Practising English, or Putting Spin on a Ball

Practising Techniques

Thus far, you have learned and practised the basics of pocket billiards. With the straight-on shots, at varying speeds, you learned how to master the art of pocketing colored balls, either directly or indirectly. You acquired a feel for cradling the cue stick, warm-up strokes, aiming, and shooting. If you had everything lined up but the ball did not follow the path you intended it to take, it was most likely because you did not hit the cue ball straight-on but rather slightly off to the side. But now let us use this advanced technique purposefully.

Using English has always fascinated the novice player, and it is indeed astounding that a cue ball seems to develop its own dynamic, changing its path after contact with an object ball, as if guided by the hand of a ghost. But let us not forget that a billiard ball, too, must follow the laws of physics—even if they are difficult to recognize and calculate. Here, too, as with everything else, "Practice makes perfect."

Practising Forward Spins, Back Spins, and Stop Balls

The forward spin, back spin, and stop ball can be considered the simple forms of English. To refresh your memory, a cue ball with a forward spin is struck above the middle; with a back spin, it is struck below the middle; and, with a stop ball, it is struck also below the middle, but quickly and hard.

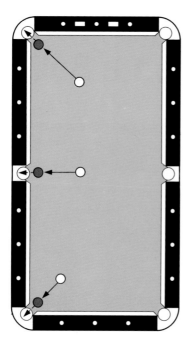

Exercise 15.

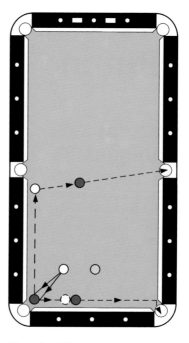

Exercise 16.

Exercise 15

Try to pocket the object balls, as indicated above, with the stop-ball technique, first from close up and then lengthening the distance as you go on. This exercise can also be used for practising the back-spin shot.

Exercise 16

Pocket ball 1 with forward spin into the right corner pocket. In order to avoid pocketing the cue ball as well, make sure that you do not aim at the middle but at either the left or right of the pocket. This will cause the cue ball to run along the rail after contact and avoid accidental pocketing. Practise both: aiming at the right and the left edges of the pocket. That way, you can attempt to position your cue ball for the next shot—either aiming ball 2 into the corner pocket or ball 4 into the left side pocket.

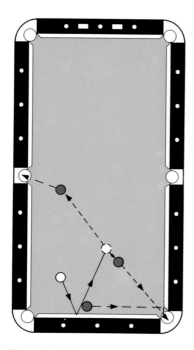

Exercise 17.

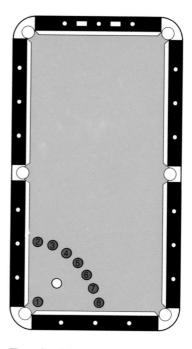

Exercise 18.

Exercise 17

If you were able to successfully complete the previous exercise, practise the same strategy for the back-spin shot, with the goal of achieving a better position for subsequent shots.

Pocket ball 1 with the back-spin shot. Now try to pocket ball 2 across the rail, while trying, at the same time, to achieve optimum cue-ball position for playing ball 3. This exercise can be expanded by striking balls with the stop ball in the corner pocket and then continuing by hitting ball 4 in the side pocket.

Exercise 18

This is another exercise for practising forward-spin, back-spin, and stop balls. Position the colored balls as indicated in the drawing above. First, pocket ball 1, while, at the same time, establishing good cue-ball position for ball 2. Now put ball 1 and the cue ball back in their original positions. Continue the exercise, always pocketing ball 1 first, while, at the same time, establishing position for pocketing ball 3, and so forth. First use stop balls, then forward spins, and last back spins.

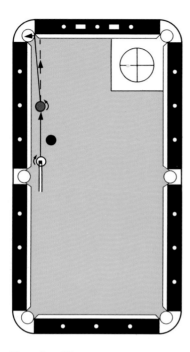

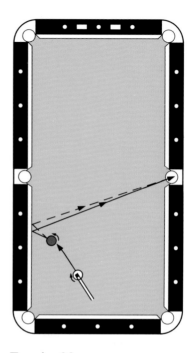

Exercise 19.   *Exercise 20.*

Practising Off-to-the-Side Strokes

In order to properly apply the off-to-the-side stroke, let's recall briefly the "law of opposites."

If a ball with English hits another ball it will cause that ball to spin in the opposite direction. This means that the object ball does not follow the (imaginary) extended line drawn from the point of impact through its middle, but, rather, it is deflected slightly in the direction of the spin. This has to be taken into account.

Exercise 19
Here, the cue ball and object ball are lined up in a straight line. Playing the object ball at an angle is prevented by a third ball. As the cue ball strikes the object ball on the left side, the object ball reverses the spin on the right and it is forced into the left corner pocket.

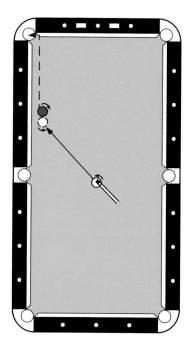

Exercise 21.

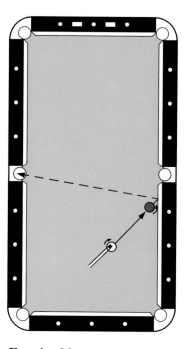

Exercise 22.

Exercise 20

It will become clear that you must not only take into consideration the behavior of the ball after rail impact but also the direction of the path the ball will travel. Here, move the point of impact on the rail forward a little more. How much will depend on how fast the ball is spinning and how forceful the stroke.

Exercise 21

Off-to-the-side shots can also be used in the case of a frozen object ball. The cue ball must be played so that it makes contact with the rail and the object ball simultaneously. The object ball will run along the rail into the pocket.

Exercise 22

In addition, you may also make use of a wider angle of completion, using the counter-spin (here, transferred to the object ball).

55

Making Use of What You Have Learned: More Advanced Shots

that the cue ball's direction will divert at an angle of 90 degrees. If an opponent's ball is blocking the direct path to your object ball, you might want to consider using a detour in order to pocket a second choice first and then concentrate on your first choice—*before* you risk playing off the rail. Also, consider if a carom will be an advantage, for instance, in playing for position for the next shot, or, in a Nine Ball game, in the opportunity of pocketing the winning 9 ball.

Caroms and Combination Shots

Playing with a second ball means playing billiards on a higher level. Nevertheless, an experienced player will always keep in mind the following basic rule: that the direction of the path in which the object ball will travel is always the (imaginary) line from the point of impact straight through the middle of the ball and

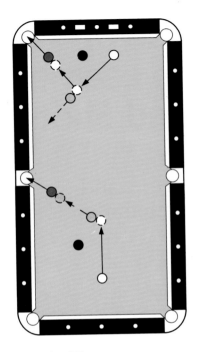

Exercise 23.

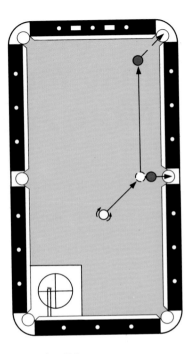

Exercise 24.

Practice for Caroms and Combination Shots

Exercise 23

Here, you have two different situations, in which a second ball is used as "the rail," and the second ball takes over the role of the cue ball.

Exercise 24

In this case, we have one object ball sitting directly in front of the side pocket and another object ball in front of a corner pocket. Hit a forward-spin shot with a left spin, but don't use too much force. It is sufficient to just gently nudge the first object ball. The diversion of the path of the cue ball lets it roll straight towards the second ball, pocketing it in the corner.

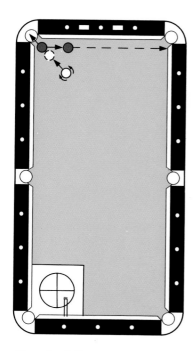

Exercise 25.

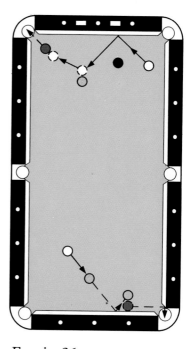

Exercise 26.

Exercise 25

This is an example of an opposite hit: the back-spin shot with a right spin.

Exercise 26

Test and practise playing off the rail for caroms and for combination shots.

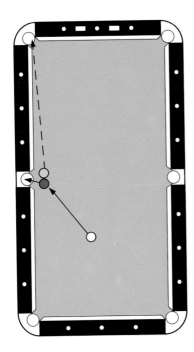

Exercise 27.

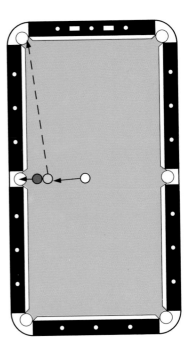

Exercise 28.

Frozen Balls

When two balls are frozen and one of them is the actual object ball, you are faced with a difficult situation. The following examples are of such standard situations that you should practise them whenever possible. Of course, you can position balls any way you wish, and, from real game situations, you will get many other ideas of what is possible.

Playing Frozen Balls

Exercise 27

This is a situation similar to the one in exercise 23. Two balls are frozen in front of a side pocket. Try to hit the red ball at an angle of about 45 degrees; this way, the red ball will sink into the side pocket and the grey ball will be deflected and sink into the upper left corner pocket.

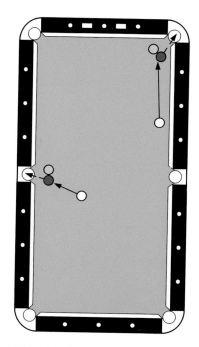

Exercise 29.

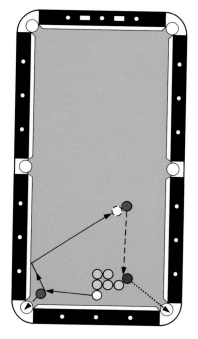

Exercise 30.

Exercise 28

In this situation, it will be easy to pocket both balls into the side pocket with a very gentle stroke. However, you can also try to hit the grey ball slightly to the left; it will force the red ball into the side pocket, and the grey ball will continue running and sink into the corner pocket.

Exercise 29

A similar situation is shown here. This is a basic rule you should try to remember: If two balls are frozen to each other and the carom line points directly to the middle of a pocket, the ball closest to the cue ball can be pocketed. But always play this ball on the side that is away from the pocket.

Exercise 30

Exercise 30 is well suited to practise this situation. Hit ball 1 into the right corner pocket, playing for cue-ball position so that ball 2 can be pocketed into the left corner pocket.

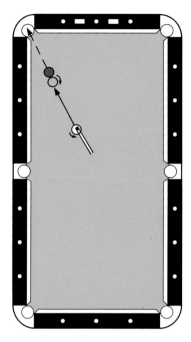

Exercise 31.

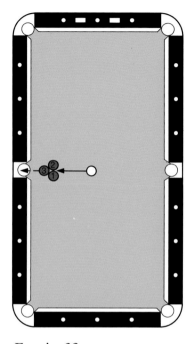

Exercise 32.

Exercise 31

Both frozen balls are not directly in front of the corner pocket but positioned slightly off to the left. This difference can be compensated for with a right-spin shot. The grey ball is hit on the outside, the left side, which creates a strong left spin. This "correction" pushes the red ball slightly to the right, which will result in the ball rolling into the left pocket.

Exercise 32

This is another good exercise for practising accurate aim. Three balls are frozen in front of a side pocket. If balls 1 and 2 are hit simultaneously and with equal force, ball 3 can easily be pocketed.

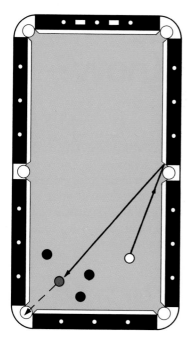

Exercise 33.

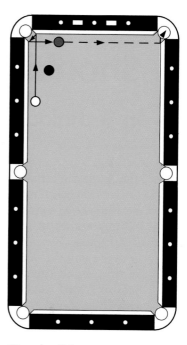

Exercise 34.

Corner Balls

Playing a ball across a corner successfully seems to be almost a matter of luck. You must aim with the greatest precision, but, more often than not, these situations are so confounded that most shots are unpredictable.

However, if you have some time left after you've practised the other exercises, include this technique as well.

Hitting Corner Balls

Exercises 33 and 34
These two exercises are for practising corner balls. In the first instance, try to aim at the corner of the side pocket in such a way that the cue ball bounces off the railing and, avoiding the ball of the opponent, hits the red ball into the corner pocket.

The second shot represents true artistry. The cue ball is played off both edges of the left corner pocket before it hits the red ball for the right corner pocket.

63

What Else Should You Know?

Tips on Techniques

At this point, you have learned and practised the basic and more advanced techniques of pocket billiards. But one aspect cannot be emphasized enough: the importance of getting accustomed to proper stance and proper grip and swing of your cue stick. Make sure, at all times, that your left hand is placed securely on the table, providing a solid bridge so that your cue stick won't slip. You might want to engage in the help of a partner to assure yourself that you aren't using a pumping motion with your right arm. The movement of the stick is generated at the elbow, and the stick should only move in the direction that you intend it to move. Also, remember not to strike with too much power. Powerful strokes, particularly for beginners, result in inaccurate shots, like sending the cue ball in the wrong direction or giving it wrong English.

It is also important to stay with your stroke. Don't straighten up your upper body right away, but, rather, stay in your striking position for a moment and, with your eyes, follow the path of the cue ball and object ball. Try to fix on the contact point made by both balls. This is the only way to learn what mistakes you might have made or to get validation for the correctness of your shots. If you take all of this to heart, nothing will stand in your way of playing a successful game.

Tips on Tactics

Pocket billiards is a game of tactics. It is a typical beginner's mistake to concentrate only on the shot immediately in front of him or her and ignore the position of the other balls on the table. Good players "read" a situation. They analyze the position of all the balls on the table and plan subsequent strokes accordingly.

You should try as early as possible (start when you are practising techniques) to play for position. Always think two or three steps ahead. During your practice sessions, once the different methods of hitting the cue ball have become a little more routine, start putting more emphasis on achieving ball position. With this, as with everything else you need to learn, start simply and then work yourself up to the finer points. In other words, don't place too many balls on the table in the beginning. We recommend practising with games of straight pool and Nine Ball, since, in both cases, you play every ball.

When practising, mark the position of the cue ball and object ball with chalk and play several different alternatives from the same position. This will sharpen your awareness, and you won't find yourself getting stuck with just one solution to a particular situation.

Also, practise safety shots—defense shots in which a player tries to leave the cue ball in such a position that the opponent faces a difficult or impossible shot. There will be times when you won't be able to pocket a ball without making a mistake or committing a foul. Try to execute a legal stroke, but focus your attention on positioning your ball so that it is your opponent who will be in a difficult position. Safety shots are required when your ball is obstructed or surrounded by an opponent's ball(s).

Try not to position your cue ball too close to the rail (unless you are hitting a safety shot!). It would not be an easy position from which to execute your next shot, and being close to the rail often does not make for a steady bridge.

Before the start of each game, the players determine who will shoot first: Each player shoots a ball from the head to the foot of the table, and the player whose ball returns closest to the head of the table starts the game. In Nine Ball and straight pool, it is an advantage to make the first shot—but only if you are sure

The Belgian billiards player and 29-time world champion, Raymond Ceulemanns, is in the top ranks for the sport. Ceulemanns is a master, both in techniques and tactics.

that you have good command of breaking techniques.

If you want to improve your game, look for an experienced partner. He or she can correct you and also give you tips and observe your game; you can learn much from such feedback.

65

Measuring Your Performance

Different Games and Their Rules

Eight Ball, Nine Ball, and straight pool are not only the most popular billiard games but also the only ones for which we have a set of *official rules* and that are played in tournaments. World-championship games are held only for Nine Ball; Eight Ball and straight pool have just European and German-championship games. The rules discussed here are in a very abbreviated form, but they should still provide you with a general understanding.

Also, please forgive us for treating "Tactical Tips" somewhat lightly. We feel that, on the one hand, an in-depth study would go way beyond the intention of this book, and, on the other hand, each player must learn to strategize from his or her own experience.

Racking for an Eight Ball game.

Eight Ball

Concept of the Game

Eight Ball, like straight pool, is a very popular game for the novice. You play with a white ball and 15 colored balls. Balls numbered from one to seven are solid-colored balls; balls numbered from nine to 15 are striped. The number-eight ball is special; it is black and is called the 8 ball. The object of the game, according to established rules, is to pocket the 8 ball. But first one player has to pocket the solid-colored balls and the other player has to pocket the striped balls. If a player pockets the 8 ball before he or she has pocketed all of his or her balls, he or she will have lost the game (with the exception of the opening shot). A player must announce which of his or her balls he or she intends to sink in which pocket.

Opening

Balls are placed in a triangular rack in the foot zone of the table. The top ball rests on the foot marker, with the 8 ball in the middle. The base of the triangle must be parallel to the foot rail. (See photo on page 66.)

Breaking takes place from the head of the table, and at least one ball must be pocketed or touch the rail. If neither one of these two things occurs, the opponent has the following options to consider:

- to continue the play, if in an advantageous position
- to repeat the break him- or herself
- to ask the opponent to repeat the break

If the 8 ball is pocketed with the break shot—and no foul has been committed—the player must repeat the break. If a foul has been committed, the opponent repeats the break or allows the player to do so.

The Game

Whatever—solid or striped—the first ball a player pockets, this becomes his or her balls; if it is a solid ball, he or she continues to play only solid balls; if striped, only striped balls. The player continues to shoot as long as he or she is pocketing a ball of his or her group. If one ball from each group has been pocketed with the break shot, the player continues to shoot and the next ball that he or she sinks into a pocket will determine which balls will be his or hers. If a player pockets one of his or her opponent's balls, this ball will remain in the pocket and the player continues his or her turn. The turn ends if a player fails to pocket a ball as he or she had announced beforehand or if he or she has committed a foul. If a player sinks a ball into a pocket without having called it out beforehand, this ball is replaced at the foot marker and he or she loses his or her turn.

Winning and Losing

A player wins the game if he or she has successfully called out and pocketed all of his or her balls in addition to the 8 ball.

A player loses the game when the following occurs:

- The 8 ball is pocketed prematurely or through a foul, or has left the table.
- The 8 ball is shot into a pocket other than the one announced.
- The white ball is pocketed together with the 8 ball, or has left the table.
- A player is unable, after three attempts, to execute a correct, faultless break.
- The player commits three consecutive fouls.
- The player exhibits unsportsmanlike conduct.

Tactical Tips

The break often determines the outcome of a game. The break stroke should be hard and forceful, unlike the strokes during the rest of the game; however, it should never be stronger or with more speed than your level of expertise allows. Only in this way will you have a chance to pocket a ball and keep your turn. In addition, a strong break will scatter the balls over the table and provide good positions from which you can play. A break that is too weak won't pocket a ball, and you will be at a great disadvantage in that the balls will have been spread out over the table ready to be played by your opponent.

If you have won the draw, only choose to break if you are certain of your break stroke. If you choose to break, make use of what is called a break cue. This cue stick is made from a particularly stiff material and is also somewhat heavier than a normal cue.

If you have a weak stroke, offer your opponent the break in the hope that he or she won't pocket a ball. Another possibility is a weak break stroke on purpose, leaving it to your opponent to unclutter the balls.

If you do decide to break, here are a few tips worth remembering: Try to make a straight-on shot and one that is as accurate as possible. Make sure you hit the head ball of the triangle dead-center. As a result, you won't transfer any English to the rest of the balls, the balls will be well dispersed, and the cue ball will return to the middle of the table.

The Game

It happens often that a player finds his or her balls surrounded by a pack of those of his or her opponent's. If that is the case, you should first try to figure out if you can sink one ball in such a way that the cue ball, on its "return trip," will break up the pack. Another possibility is to pocket one of your own balls directly. Sometimes balls are positioned at the outside of the pack in the direction of a pocket. If you can play only by way of one of your opponent's balls, make sure that you play your cue ball off the rail before making contact. If your opponent's ball is blocking the path to a pocket and there is no chance of sinking a particular ball, try to pocket your opponent's ball with one of your own, positioning your ball in front of the pocket and thus blocking your opponent. At the same time, you should attempt to strike your cue ball so that the impact either will free up some of your balls from the pack or at least create a difficult situation for your opponent. This would be the case if the cue ball is played in such a way that it comes to rest behind or in front of one of your own balls, preventing your opponent from playing one of his or hers directly. However, this strategy should only be employed when no other solution can be found to give you a better opening.

It is important to note that the 8 ball can be played in combination with your opponent's ball. In such a case, a foul is committed when the 8 ball is not pocketed where it had been announced, has not been touched by any other ball, or, after contact with the 8 ball, the other ball has not made contact with a rail.

Straight Pool

Concept of the Game

In many ways, straight pool is the least complicated billiards game. As is the case with Eight Ball, straight pool is also a call-shot game. The player must announce before each play which ball is to be pocketed in which pocket. The game is also played with 15 colored balls. For each ball a player has called out and pocketed, he or she will receive not only one point but also a point for every additional ball that is pocketed with the same shot. Balls that have been pocketed incorrectly must be returned to the foot marker.

A player continues his or her turn as long as he or she correctly pockets balls as called and has not committed

Balls racked for straight pool.

a foul. For every foul, the player loses one point and it becomes the opponent's turn. If only one colored ball is left on the table, the other 14 balls are put back on the table, with space left vacant at the tip of the triangle. The player who was playing when one ball was left on the table continues his or her turn and gets to choose which ball to hit. Two points are awarded if balls 14 and 15 are pocketed together, and the 15 balls are racked up again, just as at the beginning of the game. The player now will start where the white ball was left.

Opening

The balls are racked up with the tip of the triangle resting on the foot marker. Breaking is done from the head of the table.

Before the break, a player has the choice of either announcing a safety or call shot. A safety shot will leave the cue ball in such a position that the opponent has to contend with a difficult or impossible shot. A safety shot requires that, after the break, two colored balls and the white ball must hit the rail. If the player fails either one of these requirements, the opponent can take over or request that the break be repeated.

With the call shot, a player must announce the pocket and the object ball he or she intends to play. Failing to do so results in losing two points.

However, no points are deducted if the conditions of the safety shot are fulfilled. In such a case, it becomes the opponent's turn.

Who Wins

The winner is the player who first reaches the minimum number of points that have been agreed to prior to the game.

Tactical Tips

Straight pool, like no other game, is governed by tactics. Therefore, it is especially important to have a clear idea of the order in which you intend to pocket your balls. An experienced player will go as far as having a detailed vision of how to play the very last shot, and this may determine how he wants to play the break.

The Break

It is difficult, even for the experienced player, to pocket a ball with the break—and with a call shot, no less. Therefore, if possible, let your opponent be the one to break. But, if you must break, don't despair. You can always choose the safety shot. However, there are a few preconditions, in addition to your expertise, for this strategy to be successful.

Make sure that the balls are placed in the rack perfectly. This means that the base of the rack should be absolutely parallel to the rail and that all balls touch each other. A slight deviation can derail the effect of the break and thereby open the door for your opponent. Place the white ball at the head line (at the midpoint between the rail and the head marker). Place the ball to the right side or the left side of the table, as preferred.

Now try, with a steady, gentle stroke, to hit the outermost right ball in the first row. The point of impact should be one that is in a straight line with the rest of the balls in that row.

It is important, on the one hand, that the object ball be hit so gently that it finds its path to the rail and back. But, on the other hand, it must be strong enough so that the force of the impact will move the ball on the far left side of the row. In addition, the force must also be strong enough so that the white ball will find its way back to the head of the table. A forward-spin shot with a slight right-side spin (as shown in the drawing below) will accomplish this. This will increase the ball's forward motion after the impact of the rail.

Continuing the Game

A player, as a matter of course, should always keep in mind three important points:

1. Choose an object ball and decide whether it can be pocketed.
2. If so, determine whether you can free up another ball at the same time.
3. Keeping in mind your next shot, determine what is the best possible position for the white ball.

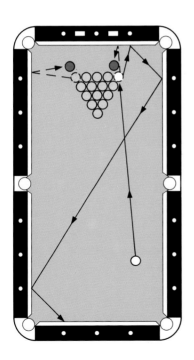

The ideal break shot for straight pool.

Point of impact for a forward-spin shot with right-side effect.

The Safety Shot

Most likely, it will not always be possible to successfully follow through on all three points. If there is no chance to pocket a ball successfully or if the situation on the table is such that you have no room for a shot, you can always fall back on a safety shot. In such a case, either the white ball or another colored ball must hit the rail. You have to call a safety shot in advance, or you will lose your turn. If a ball is pocketed in the course of the hit, that ball must be replaced on the table at the foot marker.

If a single colored ball is left on the table, you have two possibilities: Either you call a safety shot, pocket the ball (which will not count as a point), and play for position, placing the cue ball in a very difficult spot for your opponent; or you bank the colored ball, also creating a very difficult situation for your opponent. Nevertheless, keep in mind that your opponent may also respond with calling a safety shot.

Nine Ball

While Eight Ball is still considered the most popular billiards game—mainly played by beginners and those who play strictly for fun—and pool players see straight pool as the premier game of technique, some might be tempted to think that Nine Ball is a game for "insiders" only. But in America as well as all over Europe, Nine Ball has long been an integral part of the sport, even advancing, in some cases, to the number-one spot. The reason is obvious: It is a fast and therefore "spectator-friendly" game, and, as a result, it is the only billiards game that holds world-championship competitions.

The Concept

Nine Ball is played with the white ball and nine colored balls, numbered one through nine. The first ball to be played must always be the one with the lowest number. At the start of the game, naturally this is ball 1. If, in the course of a game, say, balls 1, 2, and 5 have already been pocketed, you must at least attempt to play ball 3 before pocketing any other ball.

The Break

The balls are placed in a particular order in a rhombus-shaped rack (see photo). The breaking takes place from the head field of the table. The following must happen with the break shot: Ball 1 has to be struck first, and at least one other colored ball has to hit the rail. If a player hits ball 1, it is considered legal to pocket several balls afterwards and to continue his or her turn. All balls that have been pocketed remain in their pockets. The player who has pocketed ball 9 wins the game.

If a player makes a mistake or commits a foul while breaking, the opponent has several options to consider:

- The opponent can decide to take his or her turn with the situation on the table as is, playing the white ball from the position where it was left.

- The opponent can demand that the situation on the table be improved, which means that he or she can choose any place on the table from which to shoot. If, in this situation, ball 1 is in the head field, it is placed on the foot marker.
- The third option is that either the opponent reracks the balls and breaks or asks the other player to repeat the break shot.

The Winner

The player who is able to pocket the 9 ball first has won the game.

Tactical Tips

The Break

Break with a forceful stroke. In contrast to Eight Ball and straight pool, in Nine Ball you have a good chance to pocket both corner balls of the rhombus. The most important requirement is that ball 1 be hit dead-center. Strike as hard, but also with as much control, as possible. In addition, the cue ball should always return to the middle of the table after the break shot. This is best accomplished with a stop ball. Do not strike so hard that the cue ball leaves the table or is pocketed.

A good exercise for finding "your" break stroke is the one shown in the drawing on the left. No matter from what spot on the table you make your

Balls racked for Nine Ball.

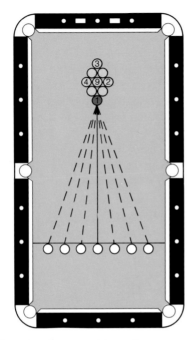

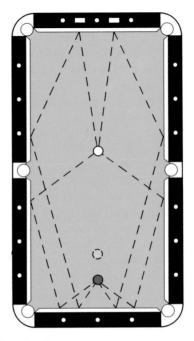

Exercise for practising the break in Nine Ball.

Exercise for practising cross-rail shots.

shot, always make sure that you gauge the force of the stroke correctly and that you strike ball 1 dead-center.

One problem that comes up in Nine Ball has to do with the difficulty of access to an object ball. Frequently, the ball you need to pocket next is hiding behind another ball, is frozen, or is in the middle of a pack. You might have no other choice than to play cross-rail shots to try to scatter the cluster. Our advice is to practise as much and as often as you can;

this will make you aware of the best possibilities when you get caught in such situations.

Five-and-Nine Ball

The Five-and-Nine game is a variation of Nine Ball. Its rules are based on Nine Ball, and the game could be considered a preliminary step to it, although not only beginners like to play it. Even so, in Europe the game is not played officially in tournaments, but it is still a welcome variation from Nine Ball.

Concept

Here, too, you play with nine balls that are, at the start, placed on the table in the shape of a rhombus. Ball 1 is placed on the foot marker, ball 9 in the middle, and ball 5 in the back. The ball with the lowest number always must be played first. If that shot is successful and another ball is pocketed, regardless of its number, the player continues his or her turn. The player loses his or her turn when he or she is either unable to hit the ball with the lowest number, has committed a foul, or could not pocket a ball successfully.

The Game

One point each is awarded to the player when he or she has successfully pocketed the 5 and 9 balls. Should this occur before the balls' actual turns, the player will still get one point each, but the balls have to be returned to the table and placed on the foot marker. If the 5 and 9 balls are pocketed when it is their turns, they remain in their pockets and the game is over. No other ball that has been pocketed is replaced on the table.

If a player is unsuccessful in hitting the ball with the lowest number—either not at all or not as the first choice—he or she has committed a foul and loses his or her turn. The opponent can now put the cue ball anywhere on the table. This can be of great value to the opponent,

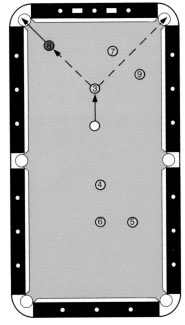

A situation in a Five-and-Nine game.

since the chances of scoring a series of consecutive points are very good.

The following is an example of a Five-and-Nine game. Player A has pocketed successfully and correctly balls 1 and 7. He does not earn any points, but he continues his turn. In his next shot, he is playing ball 3 and pocketing ball 9. This will give him one point, with the 9 ball being returned to the table. Now player A shoots a safety shot, hitting ball 3 and parking the cue ball on the rail. Now it's player B's turn. He plays ball 3 and then pockets ball 5. He also earns one point, and ball 5 is returned to the table and placed on the foot spot. If ball 9 is still at that location, ball 5 is placed close to ball 9. Now player B commits a foul, and player A gets to put the cue ball any-

where on the table. He will place the cue ball so that he can easily pocket ball 3. Next, he plays ball 4, pocketing both balls 4 and 5. He earns another point, and ball 5 is again returned to the table. With his third shot, he sinks ball 5, which now is the ball with the lowest number and therefore is not returned to the table. Player A has a 3 to 1 advantage.

In general, balls should always be pocketed in sequence. These "detours," however, are lucrative because the player is awarded extra points. In addition, they are a good way to practise caroms, banking, and playing for position. However, try to avoid committing a foul, because your opponent can position the cue ball wherever he or she chooses and you will have given him or her the advantage.

Glossary

Back spin   Shot in which the cue ball is hit below the middle so that, after impact with the object ball, it returns in the direction of its original position.

Bank   Any hit in which an object ball is rebounded from a rail.

Break   The opening shot.

Bridge   The hand that is placed on the table as support for the cue stick.

Carom   When the cue ball glances off one object ball into another.

Carom billiards   Any of several games played with two object balls and a cue ball on a table without pockets.

Chalk   Used to cover the tip of the cue stick to prevent it from slipping or sliding off the cue ball.

Combination shot   Pocketing an object ball by striking another ball with the cue ball, which then pushes the object ball into the pocket.

Cue ball   The white, unnumbered ball that is struck by the cue stick.

Cue stick   The stick used to play billiards—it is made from fine wood, is about 55 inches long, and a small piece of leather covers the tip.

Direct hit   Hitting an object ball square in its center.

Eight Ball   A type of billiards game in which one player plays with solid-colored balls and the other with striped balls—in order to win the game, after a player has successfully pocketed his or her own balls, the 8 ball must be pocketed.

English   Creating a spin on a ball by striking it to the right or left of the central point.

Forward spin   Shot in which the cue ball is hit above the middle so that it continues to follow the object ball after impact.

Frozen   When the object ball is touching another colored ball, the cue ball, or a rail.

Indirect hit   Or cross-rail shot—cue ball hitting the rail before making contact with the object ball.

Mechanical bridge A stick with a notched plate at the end, used when the normal hand bridge is not sufficient to make a shot.

Miscue When the cue stick slips from the cue ball, resulting in a faulty shot.

Nine Ball A billiards game played with nine balls—balls must be played in numerical order, and the object of the game is to pocket the 9 ball.

Object ball The ball to be shot or pocketed with the cue ball.

Safety shot A shot whereby a player tries to leave the cue ball in such a position that the opponent is faced with a difficult or impossible shot.

Snooker A billiards game played on a larger table, with balls and pockets that are smaller than is customary for the other games. It is one of the most popular games in England—it's even more popular than soccer!

Stance The way you position and hold your body when playing pool, involving solid footing, relaxed cradling and aiming of the cue stick, and holding your chin in line with the cue stick.

Stop ball Shot in which the cue ball is hit below the middle quickly and with force so that it remains on the spot where it struck the object ball.

Straight pool A game that is played by announcing each shot in advance and earning one point for every successfully pocketed ball— generally, the game is played to 100 or 125 points.

Table The table used for playing pocket billiards has six pockets, its surface is made of slate (at one time made of marble) and is covered with woolen cloth, and the rails bordering it are made of hard rubber—typically 4 feet by 8 feet and 32 inches high.

Technical foul Deliberately playing the ball of the opponent, pocketing the cue ball, and letting clothing touch a ball are all considered technical fouls.

Index

Metric Conversion

Inches to Millimetres and Centimetres MM—millimetres CM—centimetres						
Inches	MM	CM	Inches	CM	Inches	CM
⅛	3	0.3	9	22.9	30	76.2
¼	6	0.6	10	25.4	31	78.7
⅜	10	1.0	11	27.9	32	81.3
½	13	1.3	12	30.5	33	83.8
⅝	16	1.6	13	33.0	34	86.4
¾	19	1.9	14	35.6	35	88.9
⅞	22	2.2	15	38.1	36	91.4
1	25	2.5	16	40.6	37	94.0
1¼	32	3.2	17	43.2	38	96.5
1½	38	3.8	18	45.7	39	99.1
1¾	44	4.4	19	48.3	40	101.6
2	51	5.1	20	50.8	41	104.1
2½	64	6.4	21	53.3	42	106.7
3	76	7.6	22	55.9	43	109.2
3½	89	8.9	23	58.4	44	111.8
4	102	10.2	24	61.0	45	114.3
4½	114	11.4	25	63.5	46	116.8
5	127	12.7	26	66.0	47	119.4
6	152	15.2	27	68.6	48	121.9
7	178	17.8	28	71.1	49	124.5
8	203	20.3	29	73.7	50	127.0